I0517803

Diary of a False Assassin

Poems By

Anne Leigh Parrish

DIARY OF A FALSE ASSASSIN

Copyright © 2024 Anne Leigh Parrish

All Rights Reserved.

Published by Unsolicited Press.

First Edition.

No part of this book may be used or reproduced in any manner whatsoever without written permission except in the case of brief quotations embodied in critical articles or reviews. People, places, and notions in these poems are from the author's imagination; any resemblance to real persons or events is purely coincidental.

For information contact:

Unsolicited Press

Portland, Oregon

www.unsolicitedpress.com

orders@unsolicitedpress.com

619-354-8005

Cover Design: Kathryn Gerhardt

Editor: S.R. Stewart

Photography: Anne Leigh Parrish

ISBN: 978-1-963115-20-8

To John, Bob, Lacey, Lauren, Sam, Frida, and Tsuga

Acknowledgments

"A List of Things That Are Yellow"
Feminine Collective

"After That"
Scapegoat Review

"Cardigans, c. 1962"
Product Magazine

"Cause and Effect"
Feminine Collective

"Denial of Our Plainness"
Sunlight Press

"Diary of a False Assassin"
Feminine Collective

"Frog-Girl Goes to Camp"
Product Magazine

"Glide"
talking about strawberries all of the time

"How Things End"
talking about strawberries all of the time

"Intelligence"
Feminine Collective

"Lifting Brightness"
Sunlight Press

"Methow Valley"
Dipity Literary Magazine

"Peony"
Dipity Literary Magazine

"San Diego County"
Dipity Literary Magazine

"Stoning the Lake"
Scapegoat Review

"Today, June 24, 2022"
talking about strawberries all of the time

"Touched by Rain"
talking about strawberries all of the time

"Twenty Years"
Feminine Collective

"Uninvited"
talking about strawberries all of the time

Contents

Diary of a False Assassin

Blue

Walk down the blue road
And into the blue light
All around you, this color
Runs your heart, and the whole
Damned world

Sea and sky
Your veins before they bleed red
Moods and stones
The dog you took care of once,
'Member?

Strength
Survival
Your own eyes, more or less

Go toward this color, that hangs in
Green branches like an afterthought

A fancy dressing,

Or really, upon a closer look

A harder truth

Surrender

Mixed on a palette

Caressed and smudged

We've no choice but to blend

Assimilate, lose ourselves,

Surrender to greater numbers and hues

And when we've lost all sense of who

We once were, we find we've made

A dull mass of brown or gray,

Neutral, easy on the eye, ask any decorator

Trying to stage a house for sale

Is that what racists fear? The loss of white

Skin? Or the sameness of tone that would make it

Hard to be in charge, pull the trigger, tie the rope?

Denial of Our Plainness

You fade from view
Leave a hint of mauve and green
We're showgirls
Platinum hair
Pencil skirts in the daylight
Not much on stage
Guys and dolls

You hand me the coleus to transplant
Its roots dangle like lost thoughts
White border on its leaves
The color of a
Winter moon

You choose pearls plucked
From a warm sea
Pink will never be mauve
Gray only touches green
How dear, that strange desire tinged with blue

We dress for dinner

I choose black for its slimming effect

You go with a red skirt and green shoes to

Celebrate the season

The denial of our plainness

Softened by the sky's purple song

Lifting Brightness

Where the road bends west, the sky opens
And the trees stand down for a while

Its light says it hangs over water

You know what I mean by that

A lifting brightness

Not like a smile, more like
An idea of how things might be, or
Were in an easier time

I love that wide stretch above us
How it invites us to something better
To *be* better, in ourselves

Cardigans, c. 1962

Oh, those glamour girls with their cardigans

Worn, but not worn,

Draped on soft shoulders, arms still bare

Sleeves hang, waiting to be filled

Like the ladies, themselves

Is that what they're trying to say?

And when they slip their arms through for warmth

Or convenience (who wants loose sleeves hanging around,

     anyway)

Are they too busy, too practical to be bothered with love?

Glide

She was a Hoosier

From the Latin Quarter

Went by Velma, then Angelique

Pinned up her hair

Bought a patent leather belt (red)

Squeezed her swollen feet

Into patent leather heels (also red)

It's okay to reinvent yourself

Especially when the first

Version's not so great

But sooner or later, the hair comes down,

The belt and shoes slip off

(Thank God, they hurt like hell)

But that little make-believe

Leaves a touch of joy in the eye

Just knowing you can,

For a little while,

Glide through the world

As someone else

Flying to Maui

Let's sit in this small cozy space
Ours alone
No one joins
No one gets to say

The sea below folds and winks
Living its own life
Full of fish and sunken ships
No care for us

Clouds gather, holding all the light and shadow
We've ever seen
Yet their absence would ease our worry
About the bumps and jolts we
Swallow with our California cabernet

The blue below greens and grays, broken
By the white tips of waves

The island offers emeralds we didn't expect

Azure water, black sand (when we track it down)

The red and white orchids along the

Path draw the eye, stir the heart, and

Remind us how weary we've become

Methow Valley

Whisper up the valley
Nudge the branch where the sparrow
Claims a perch

Calm the fretful horse
Tethered to the fence

Soften the sharp scent of flame on wood
Bring twilight on feathered clouds
Drop violet gold over folded hills

Offer dreams to the sleepless
Grant them the river's joy
Sliding sweetly over rocks
Smoothed by her toil
Long ago

Mount Audubon

The ascent took hours

Trees thinned

Disappeared

Not much to say about rocks, except

They're hard on feet and ankles

Wind—how do we remember it?

Strong

Cold

Sudden

There, not there

Perhaps capricious is better

At the top, a cairn

In the cairn, a note

I am here, or *I made it*, or something

To the east, the trek we just made

The prairie reached away

The Earth's curve visible

At thirteen thousand feet

The sky, purple

To the west,

Folded peaks

Snow, boulders

Like staring down into the ocean

From a ship at night

Knowing it could claim you

With one false step

All that time to climb, so little time to linger

We must start our descent now

To be home by nightfall

Splendid Anguish

Sunset behind the mountain range promises and denies

What glorious, unique, impossible to reckon

Arrangement of rock—incline and descent—is now

Turning pink?

Tomorrow we begin again the

Splendid anguish of adoring the

Failing light while yearning to

Be where the sun hangs high

San Diego County

Slender twisted trunks and flat, fluttery leaves
The eucalypts bend toward the light, as if
The sinking sun would pull them into the sea

Rain so scant the fall of a moment
Brings a glisten and shine to the yucca and jade

Fire passed here
Blackened
Singed

Spared stone mansions
On the ridgetops
Full of light, for now

Each season could be the one
To hollow out and tear down
Leaving behind shadows and soot

Remarkable, too

In their way

Over Arizona

I know you from the light,
Leached shades,
Pale, tan, rocky

Which isn't a shade, except here

Canyon's river is low and narrow
The path cut over eons

Where it catches the sun, it
Gives back a diamond

Big Thompson, 1976

In dry land they
Pray for rain
Back home, rivers swell

You consider this
From your perch on Flagstaff Mountain
Prairie rolls east
Rockies stand west

Two canyons over,
The sky gathers
In a lavender knot

You want a wild show
Lightning's dance
Storms out here never disappoint

In the morning news comes

Of a water wall

Some escaped, most didn't

How lucky you were to be above it all

Loving a sky no less beautiful for the

Curse it held

Country Living

We don't know them, not really
Their names, sure, from the mailbox
And the list of contact info
Passed around as we reckoned how to
Replace the private road connecting us
Ridged and pocked from being
Laid wrong in the first place

We speculate
Guess
Look out their windows
Sleep in their beds
Give them happiness we don't have
More money
Better vacations
Peace of mind

Now and then a muffled shout
As we pass with the dog

A tear-stained face disappears

As the garage door lowers

Was it any different in the city?

More people around = less focus

Fewer people = intense observation

Or maybe it's not them, it's us

Out here in the country

Where everything feels bigger,

More important

Loneliness, most of all

By Turns

One small stone shifts
Under the weight of what
Takes a lifetime to forget

Now it's all back

You can't remove it, or build around it

Everything you do depends on how it's balanced,
How long it cares to sit in a single
Spot

Before gathering damp loosens the earth and
Sends it to a new, uneasy
Stead

There are no homes in this life

Only places we carve out of fields and trees

Under stars that rise or still

By turns

Resting on that single stone

Poised, met by a silent wish to

Hold fast and

Resist the smallest nudge

In a place you can

Claim and find again

When nightmares end

Lost and Found

The clip sits like a shell on the bathroom ledge

Freed from the hair it held,

It now holds itself

Isn't that the gift of being left?

The loser chose it for its calming green

And its wide, easy clutch

But the moment is neither easy nor wide

As the flight is called

So, the hair lies loose and the clip

Waits for another finder

Venn

We're a beautiful Venn diagram, you say, just
Look how we overlap!

I'm given the center, where I
Meet my child and partner
You, that is
Both of you

There's nothing in the diagram that isn't just me
I alone am not there
I know you're okay with that
To you, it makes perfect sense

I'm defined by the two of you

Would you be okay if you were in the center, smothered?

Put me on the edge and I'll grab a passing star

We'll ask nothing of each other, that star and I

Our intersection will be spectacular

And mercifully brief

Universe

You have to look away for it to happen
In that little blindness, things turn on

Think of the watched pot

Turning off is an event, too
Just as hard to nail down

One's life—existence—is always connecting and
Hanging up on everything around

Stars within us shift, wink out

Each of us is a universe, full of darkness
Graced now and then
By a brilliant point of light

I'll Show You

Bargain with me, why don't you?
Don't tell me how it's all gonna be

Who put you in charge, anyway?
Takes two to tango
And to make a zygote

You don't remember me?
So, why are you pushing me around?

You're just that kind of guy
Bellow first, whisper later

But you tire so quickly
While I carry on
Fix your grievous fault

Work with me, not against me

But if you're too lazy/scared/arrogant/blind

I'll show you how to labor, overcome, be humble, and see

How It Will Always Be

Her bare feet slap the asphalt
His sneakers stride in silence

Yelling, of course
Ugly words

He won't slow down
She can't go faster

This is how it will always be

She wants justice
He wants to run

But won't

He faces her
She says her piece

You made me bleed

A List of Things That Are Yellow

Sunlight

Egg yolk

Daffodils

A rare diamond

Amber

Anything not alive

Our house

A sickly skin tone

Bruises

The car you owned when we met

Butter

Lemons

Fallen leaves

Pineapples

The tie you tried to strangle me with

The straw in the ice water they gave me to drink at the police
      station

Your madness

My fear in staying so long

Yield

The young draw such hard lines
Slam doors until hinges unhinge
Build walls
Trade one prison for another
When the world shuts them out

Sun strengthens
Overcomes damp
Dries what ran to rot
In month after wet month

It takes years to open and awaken,
Yield to the process of becoming
Part of everything, everywhere

How to impart that when
Walls tumble, it brings not surrender
But joy?

48

Do You Remember?

Do you remember sledding at night on the golf course?

The boys held lights to show us the way

We made our own way

Do you remember the river down below?

Rushing black and bright under the moon

Like us

We two

We went too fast on that sled

It veered

We, too

I leaned toward the water and didn't go in

Because you held onto me

Do you remember how that felt?

Grateful Dead

The soundtrack in this bar is eclectic—
Whoa, here comes Elvis
Weren't we just listening to The Police?

Now it's The Dead!

Sappy, syrupy

The stuff of our collective histories

Once woozy with hope
We're now wizened, wise in the ways of the world

Just ask that couple over there
Her face is wistful
His, hard

They're realigning around a shifted

Vantage point

No one's young anymore

We accept grief and failure

As easily as the startling beauty

Of the heather's first bloom

All things are not equal in their power over us, though

That music, from so long ago,

Can still hold sway

Dancing Off

Pleasures overtake us, we can't keep up

Some go

Some are kept, but smaller, so much less delightful

Youth is heady and desperate

Age is a struggle to stand on one foot

Just when you balance, you tilt

Cogs loosen

This is how we glide away from the world

Dancing off

Step by clumsy step

Reverie

Flames in the corner
Fireplace or wood stove
Peril or delight
Watch and wait

Can't make the phone work
Illegible keys
No dial tone

Fire's hotter now

Snow rushes through an open window
Swirls into the fireplace

(See? it *is* a fireplace)

Flames drop but keep dancing
Just like me

Dream Shadow

If the dream shadow comes, it's always right before sleep

When what danced the night before

Cuts loose, opens a door to a room

I'm about to enter, reminding me what the

Color scheme was, who laughed first

Now shadows flicker after lunch, while I work

Through the afternoon

Boundary softens, the process jumps its wall

Has time forever altered?

I hope so

Who doesn't want to be seduced by the unknown?

Birds of Prey

What name, yours?

Feather color? Arrival time?

Morning scalp bloodied, raw

Nightmare party

Carried in her talons over seas and flat earth

I drop into the torturer's hand

Just a minion, that noble bird

Good for errands, rending flesh

When the torturer tires, the bird doesn't come

Yet I lie awake

Waiting for the sound of her wings

The taste of my own blood

How Things End

Everything has a center
Everything, a lost edge

It feels like we're about to disappear

So, we cling to that center,
To what we think we know

Never realizing that
How things end might
Matter more than
How they begin

Uninvited

I love you because you love me

No better reason

Golden magnet

Sweet wine

Honeyed words

So easily sung

This is what we're born to

Seek/hunger for/claim

Like rage, love lands

Unannounced

Uninvited

Just like fear

And it's fear we answer as we

Weigh love's worth,

Ponder the cold cell

Our hearts become

Should we shun it, make excuses,

Run off into that long,

Predictable, uneasy

Quiet called loneliness

The Clouds Look Down

Yesterday, the clouds float south to north
   Today, they race the other way
   Changeable

Yesterday, they watch us
   Chuckle about the neighbor cutting grass
   Guy can't mow a straight line

Today, they don't linger, but
   See our woe, hear our silence and
   Feel grateful for how they can
   Pull apart and regroup at will

Their pity moves them along,
   Opens the sky's blue dome to
   Whatever we hope to see there,
   Hungry for peace and perfection

Moment by Moment

Watch the seedhead drift
The dandelion it once was, gone
No thoughts of past things
Only these little moments
Falling, rising on a gust

Just as those airy stalks touch down, you
Look away, hungry for the future

There it is,
Another seedhead set free to
Meet, then join the constant,
Turning Earth

Remember Me

Remember me as twilight

Falls and gently claims the day

Dread not the velvet darkness,

Coming softly without fail

Observe the ebbing tide,

Rejoice in its faithful rise

Know absence is but brief,

When love begins again

Intelligence

You think time stops because you figure something out

Like how your ex-bf sings for tiny women and since you're tall
His love for you was never true
Despite what he swore, through crocodile tears, as he
Pinned you to the wall

Or later, at the window with a wide-eyed baby in your arms,
The city's midnight bones tease the idea . . . men build everything
        you see—
Phone poles, streets, bridges, because you—women—do this,
This child

And that these revelations stop time

Insight only hits the pause button, then you go on wondering
        what's going to happen next

A bright light in a crowded sky
Needing a pattern only you can see

General to Specific

A single hurt speaks for all the rest

Tonight's socks on the floor
Are a mountain built day after day

My headache is a line of red foreheads,
Refusing your touch, year after year

We talk of people we know
Their broken homes
Their slipped-off rings and
Grieve the general loss of love

Now, we speak in specific terms,
To the end we can't escape

The time has come for us to leave this place
This empty bed
This life

So Many Years

A party, two beers, sex in the den
Wow—so great!
>   It wasn't

Weeks later, at another party, in another house
Across another noisy room,
>   Where assignations/hookups/affairs/maybe
>   One eventual moderately successful long-term
>>   relationship
>   Mixed and churned toward a variety of possible outcomes

I saw you not see me,
Then you did

Your gaze brought me . . .
Nothing

Forgotten?
Or just canceled?

That blindness in your eye

Made me blind, too

So many years until I saw myself again

Steel

Be the sweet-girl, sexy-girl

Everyone loves

The good-time girl

They steal you

Steel yourself

Don't dance

Stand on the riverbank

When the sun shines through the

Feathers of the red-tailed hawk

Know you are that brightness

As light softly fades

Slip away unseen

They're blind to you now

Be free

Cause and Effect

Tell her she's a witch, she'll cast a spell
Say she's a queen, she'll rule the roost

Call her ugly, she'll lie in bed
Praise her beauty, she'll dare the sun

Whisper she's stupid and she'll flunk the test
Insult her limp and she'll stand still

Call her temptress, she'll wear a sheet
Name her whore, her body goes cheap

Say she's a person and her choices have weight
Show her respect and she'll build a world

Today, June 24, 2022

Today, when the patriarchs turn women into livestock
Here you are, radio on high, giving forth

Your nose ring catches the light,
Your shaved head says *don't touch*

Crank up the volume
That's rockin' music you've got there

You won't hide underground, lie in your own blood, die
Not today—
Today you sing for all you're worth

Ancestry.com

Welcome to the family tree
Arabian Peninsula?
Gotta be that Armenian grandmother
Trucking around the Ottoman Empire

No Irish, despite what you heard growing up
Lots of Scots and English, though

You have the body of a sturdy peasant,
Good for hauling wood, forking hay,
Bearing hordes of children

One in three women used to die that way
Some still do

Then, you could change your mind
Before the quickening
Now, you can't

Without choice, you're a ghost

Haunting a country that thinks you're a cow

Your ghosts have found their homelands

While you are homeless,

Weeping for your sisters,

Hungry for a homeland of your own

The Flipside

Start with the leaves

In the windlift their underside is pale

An impression of fluttering brightness

[Yes, yes, you think—Monet's playbook/source material]

Air up a woman's skirt

A view into some forbidden

Popular

Necessary

Legend

Because facts are sometimes

Distasteful

Unpalatable

Downright disgusting

Look at that vagina tear

Pushing out the parasite

These are the days of forced birth

No softness

No euphemism

We used to say in the family way

Whose family?

Who got in the way?

Some love

Husband

Stranger

Rapist

Sperm donor

Friend with benefits

Pushy one-way dead-end-street dude

Or the best thing that ever happened to you

Sometimes the flipside is an upside

Just depends on where you look

Changing Luck

Knowing you're gone hits like a white-hot migraine
The lead-up is a quickening, not in the womb, but in the heart

In my mind's eye, you drape gently on my old-lady neck
Don't argue—this truth cannot be unhinged

Blue-green turquoise—my eye color
Shot with silver lines
(Which lie in wait, ready to spring)
With a flimsy silver clasp
Were they mined in spring?

Nowhere to be found
Drawer after drawer searched
Removed, contents apologized to
Why should the Taxco silver choker find itself upside down?
Its reputation tarnished
It, too, in that drawer, so long ignored

You're gone!

Where? The hotel in Arizona, left on the bathroom ledge

Wouldn't they have called? Offered to mail it back?

What if the maid claimed it for herself?

Wears it out now with her new man?

The thought of those stones, lying on someone else's skin

Talk about white-hot rage

But consider the pleasure this brings her

The sense that finally, her luck has changed

You can get another necklace, after all

This treasure is the only one she may ever own

Like the Snow

Trees dress like ballerinas

Rooflines assume grace

The beauty of softened edges

And dead sound

Each snowflake is unique

Maybe the same is true of people

Thus, each is highly prized

So, why are you pushed, slapped, insulted, ignored

Told to disappear, ordered to reappear?

Be like the snow

Silent

Lovely

Frequent

Cold

Separation

All we know of winter
Is the rain drip from the branch
All the life we cannot see
Lies in the stripped-down limb

Watch the very spot
Where the leaf dried,
Curled and let go months before

Wait for the greening shoot

Sit by the fire while the night
Bears down
Hear the clock tick, the furnace
Run, the bare branch scrape glass

Your face the same
Your eyes, too
Yet something stirs behind them

Unseen, ineffable

Until the season moves

Taking you with it

Once, all my winters ended in spring

As I ended in you

Now, I begin in mist and rising light

Alone

Lavinia Studios

Fog

Stills wind

Mutes light

There's a sun up there somewhere

Tallest evergreen branches fade

As if drained of their life force

A week of fog oppresses, some say

But what if it swaddles us,

Offers comfort and love?

Consider the heart that looks at nature

As a mother

How sad and clichéd

Or perhaps it knows, when we suspend

Our disbelief, how things really are

Feels a deeper truth

In ordinary things

Tulips

At first, they hold together
Stems straight, like pickets in a
New fence

After one day, they
Soften, bend

An opening, of sorts
This reach to the light

It's what plants and flowers do
Only tulips do it so well

Ballerinas in a vase

Come and Go

Winter fades every year and every year we're
Stunned by the rising green and blue

As if we've never seen it
Never been grateful, not this grateful, anyway

Memory is short, often false
Darkness becomes forever

No logic will light it

Seasons need no logic

They lift and fall like a woman's happiness
Granted, then denied by a breath of wind

Peony

The peony spreads underground

Those words suggest a movement

    Either to build or destroy

    Both, really

    Can't do one without the other

    Unless by building one is

    Adding to, not replacing

The image is not political

    What *is* political in nature?

    Survival, conquering, besting

    Sounds political, if you filter it

    Through the lens of human history

Which I'd rather not

Each spring brings more shoots and each

Gives a blossom

The heat dome didn't ruin it

Nor the foot of snow

A resilient gorgeous plant

Plotting to take over the garden

Winter Garden

I feel like the winter garden

Bare, cold

Life pushes its way through me

I'd like it to wait—

I won't lie much longer,

Resisting the planet's tilt

For now, I'm enjoying

The illusion of slumber

A slow process

Joyful silence

Rest

Without Us Knowing

Six-legged spider explores the sink
Two legs lost when it hatched

Copper-colored ladybug on the arm of
Your chair makes you wonder, too

Where are the black dots?
Those missing two legs?

Life spins new versions of itself
Without us knowing

We focus so hard on what we hope to gain,
Sometimes this feels like loss

Better to take the lovely creatures
For what they are

Even though they're not

What we expect

Revel

Reluctance

Scraped earth, mud

A shoot here, another over there

How well the moss does now

Rain drives us mad!

Let's crawl below the surface of

The pebbled ground and

Hide from the absent sun

So defeatist

We're still alive, even after decades

Of sorrow and fatigue

So, what're a few more weeks?

Nothing to do but

Wait for the whiter light to

Drape the sky

Revel when it comes

Lavinia Studios

Stoning the Lake

Let's skip stones while waves ripple the shore

Flat ones are best
Tap-tap-tap
Over the water they go, until gravity drowns them

Stone can't drown, only breathers choke

This lake won't last, you say, it's lower every day

It's just as blue, and the sunlight dances just as fast

We're the ones dying and, in our grief, stone the lake

Resurrection

Summer evening so lovely
I am lovely, too

Easy and soft
Settling in both treetop and verge

Darkness reclaimed
By folded earth, hungry to receive

Let it put forth the pink blossom
From bitterness and grief

Empty, light, it's my turn
To rise and drift

Wrongs become air
When you learn to let go

Lavinia Studios

Until Light Returns

Crows carve the banded sky while light
Slides into a desert night
Snow swirls over stone
Cold is harsh and sudden
They're left breathless, I think
As I watch from a warmer place

But that's clearly not so, given
How they swoop and rise
Their lungs labor beautifully
Giving what is asked of them

They need only to reach the next
Valley, and find a pinyon pine to
Roost in until light returns
While I'll lie sleepless,
Desperate for wings and hollow bones

Not Only

Gulls rise, fall

Hold the light

As if it were always theirs

We're jealous of

How easily they

Belong not only to

Earth and her damp churn

But to the endless glow

Of sun and sky

Joy Rising

Painted sky

Clouds glued in place

No leaf shifts its emerald plane in the dappled light

The only movement is joy

Rising, there in the summer garden

A trill escapes the sturdy throat of a robin

Balanced on the fence rail

Thickening air has found its herald

Rain falls

All goes mad

False Parable

Fallen blue feather
Lies brilliantly on the grass
In hand—turned into, then out of the light—
Hue brightens, fades
Glory becomes ordinary
This single feather is some sad parable
Of loss and a failure to thrive alone

But plumage is taken as a whole,
When the sun finds that darting bird
A missing feather means nothing
Against that sizzling sapphire flash

Gather

Light falls through trees

All that golden glow

Spread across the bloom of later summer

Gather yourself for the darker days

Sit with quiet creatures

Through the turning

Draw toward the hearth

Wear the night cloak

Bach, Not Bach

Inventions played on a guitar sound false,
Though the strings are plucked,
Like a harpsichord

If played on a piano,
We accept the hammer's strike—
The presence of a keyboard
Makes it true

What we don't know is a lie
Until we see how near it is
To what we're used to

Assign

Pitted concrete . . . Jackson Pollock in stone

Ridged asphalt . . . sand pattern left by waves

Peeling paint . . . leaves fluttering on the branch

We project what's fine within us

The inanimate and ugly take on grace

Can we not also assign beauty to others,

Treat them better, care more,

Allow them dignity and worth?

Unfolding

Is there more in me than dreams unfolding on a page?

Other ways to feast?

The camera beckons and the keyboard taunts

Even as words shine

There aren't as many years to go as I have already

    Given

    Invested

    Grieved

But plenty of time to add another light or two

Water Music

Handle's gift rises
Over the river

So stirring, so bright!

Gold coins must flow
To pen the next score

Royal patronage the game
Smile, kiss his ring

Honor the king's majesty,
Rival the grace of wings

Own Style

Francoise Gilot

Picasso's pet-turned-wife

Stellar mentee

Absorbed so much, then

Dumped the creep,

Kept painting in a Cubist vein

Which ex-hubby invented

Though Georges Braque had a hand

Didn't she want to make her own style?

Or did she figure she'd spent so long in

Angles and flattened perspective it was hers, too?

What makes something ours?

Knowledge = possession?

Maybe we never own what serves our art

Just take what we need, and

Pass it along

Transfer of Ownership

To recall something is to dream it again
That same filtered light
Falling in uneven pockets
You end up wearing
In pants that fit perfectly
Until they don't

Did it really happen, that thing with the pants?
Or has time reshaped it the way light bends around
A planet?

Whose time?
Whose planet?

The very old accept this soft edge to things
And the transfer of ownership

How do I know?

The line fades for me, too

But I still own my truths

Even as I prepare to give them away

Can't

i

Let's take this slow (ly)

What I have to say

Can't

Cant

Immanuel Kant

A spiral racetrack

Leaning into a theory of freedom but

Secured/sunk on the bottom to hold the rest up

ii

I can't love you anymore

iii

Don't come back

iv

Nothing has changed

v

Bones soften, minds sharpen, souls grow younger
Backward in time
Past the point of origin

vi

Blink out now

vii

So, I can shine forever

Stasis, As a False Concept

You never see fall's final coming of night

Nor spring's first dawn

They happen, though

So much you miss yet know is there

Always moving

Nothing holds still

Except for that space between heartbeats

But even then, blood gathers and oxygen exchanges

As false things often are

The concept of stasis is alluring—

That moment when it all just

STOPS

How to address that change is the only constant?

Ask how and for whom

Shift the balance

Aim it where it needs to go

Hard Truths

You preach patience for their ignorance,
Offer comfort for the pain they suffer

I believe too much in punishment,
Or consequences, at the very least

If you know COVID kills, yet forgo the vaccine
You're a fool
And take help another could use

You say to deny them is to ignore their humanity
I suppose you're right

Like the motorcyclist with no helmet who
Bashes his brains to smithereens
Then thousands are spent to help him speak again

You say that's it,

Everything is about help

No matter who needs it

Or why

Complexity

Green shoes to the right
Red, left
Simple sorting
Clear, clean

Yellow-green causes second thoughts
Aren't we allowed just the one
        thought?

Red russet umber
Left creeps/limps toward center
Eyes open and before too long
        blink

Complexity

No clear answers
Straight/curve

Bright/dark

On/off

How to reckon that uneasy swirl where doubt is

Carried in and out as we breathe?

Some say faith gives comfort in the face

Of unclear paths

What of reason that burns like starlight?

Always there, above us?

That we look, ask, love, and grieve = the complexity

We can't deny

Mandate ≠ conclusion

Ask, think, ask

Fear not the tangled verge

Lavinia Stuidos

123

How the Past Lives

The historian looks back,
The witness, here

Today's bleed, not the dried blood
Lifted by a trained, gloved hand
From a femur found in some deeply
Searched hinterland

You view this in a TV documentary,
Or in the picture of a magazine and
Think—wow!
How did it get there?
Who was the villain
Who, his victim?

Your mind spins like a fire wheel
Seeing how it might have been

The moment goes, as it must,

Time never stops for long

Now becomes then

Once more

Now

Everything is now

This moment

This instant

Pass your eyes over these words—

They are now

The next line is now, too

At the end, your reflection of what you have read is now

Remembering is now, even though what you remember

Took place earlier—a second ago, yesterday, last year,

Before you were born

What you see ahead—in an hour, or when bones

Crumble from age, and names can't

Find your tongue

Is now

The stone steps worn down by the pious are now

The end of time is now

Hold infinity in your heart, behind your eyes, in your fingertips

As you shuffle your cards

Everything that flashes, or gently

Leads the tawny prairie toward dawn, or

Dims bit by bit until darkness calls it home

Is now

Illuminated Manuscript

Gold leaf, peacock's tail

King, queen, swords,

Castles, stolen lands

    Days of conquest go on forever

Painted lines

Curve through time

Hunger deeper than bone

    Desperate days go on forever

Template faces

Human body an idea

Soul's awkward vessel

    Days of heaven go on forever

Sumptuous records

Rekindle beauty,

Splendor and joy

    But dying days go on forever

Without Words

Speak to me without words
Lift a hand, wipe the tear, kiss the cheek

But our language lives within
Even if it won't find the tongue

No life without words
No mind

The artist, in his deepest truth and roughest touch
Slapping yellow over ochre to sharpen its tone
Thinks, *more, like this*

My point?

What are with without our words?

The anthropologist sheds light
Ice age, tool, evolution, language = modern human

Lovekill

If eyes are windows to the soul, yours are chaos, energy unfocused

Electricity wild in your brain, though no seizure results, only rage

Maybe this has nothing to do with your head or even your heart
But a new body part only you possess

Unknown to science, absent from the lexicon
Cries out to be named

[Don't we all?]

Lovekill

Sits on the end of a rib, glows in the dark
Sets off the metal detector, baffles the radiologist
Turns your hands into fists
Words to blades
Decency to madness

What it does to me is unseen

Twenty, thirty, forty years

Of invisible rot

Cleared out now

Sturdy timbers

Stand firm

Nothing to

Feast on

So, as I've

Always done,

You must now

Go hungry

Frog-Girl Goes to Camp

Poor frog-girl with her bulging eyes
And thick-from-crying neck

Can't get the green plastic
Thread for her boondoggle

Can't ride Macey, the palomino

Fails the swim test,
Confined to the shallow end

A big frog in a small pond

Where's that prince to turn her back into a girl?

Missed his bus

You know about missed busses
And waiting in the rain for
The ride that never comes

You're like the frog-girl
Suffering life's disfigurement

Only on the inside
No tears for you

The brave face has its value
Smooth, sweet mask

Croak in private, you tell her
Never let them know

This Gift

They call you L'Anglaise for your mother tongue
But you're a Yankee born and bred

You're not used to being adopted
Fêted
Sought

Your clumsiness falls away
The limp goes, too

This modest Parisian neighborhood
Is a good place, though your mother
Despairs of it

The toilet is a horror, the
Bathtub, a vat
And the clothesline out
The kitchen window
Stops being quaint

Some sabbatical, she thinks, though

Her research goes well enough

You love it here because

You are loved by people

You never knew

You'll seek this gift all your life

And receive it once, maybe twice

Does Not Apply

Run over the grass, she says
Slip off your shoes and go

It's not allowed in that fussy city park
Low metal fences keep dogs and
Bums away

You're not a dog, nor a bum, just
A broken child of six

For a moment you have her heart,
This woman hired to watch you

She thinks urging you to cut loose
Will reassemble you

Wholeness does not apply

Shoes on, you stand at her side

Wait for her attention to shift

Leave you shadowed and vague

Forgotten

Safe

Twenty Years

Twenty years you've been gone and
That's just how long you've been dead
In life, you were gone, too
I was a pool you'd drown in
If you got your feet wet
You kept your feet dry

How hard to hold the truth
Like a bitter seed under your tongue

At the end, you spit it out

I guessed what you said before
Your tongue stilled for good

I had eyes

I said I forgave you

It was my turn to lie

I Never Thought

When the eye shadow goes on, you know it's serious

Something more to look forward to than

A stupid game of cards you won't put down

Didn't you say to drop by?

I'm not welcome here

All those turned-away faces and

Suspended conversations

Not about me, yet

Not right for my ears

There's a name for what slipped away here

But I can't recall it—

I've walked into the wrong house before

Starting with the one I was born in,

But I never thought it would be yours

Touched by Rain

The eggplant says you once held her,
Then gave her the blade

The garden cries for the cigarette butts
In her poisoned soil

You lied about smoking
You lied about everything

The shadows you cast are
Deep enough to dim a desert sun

Yet scent rides the air
First flowers touched by rain

Their kisses tell me
You're in them, too

I Know

I know why you got in the car and
Drove away
        I get it
        I do

I know why you couldn't tell me yourself,
Let me find out alone
        Waiting at the window, watching the driveway
        For your stupid French car

I know why the roofline in front—all grand Tudor peaks,
Differs from the one in back
        Which is gracious and gradual
        Japanese, almost

One face, one truth
Second face, second truth

Public, private

Reasonable, mad

Kind, cruel

Are we still talking about the house?

You could never face your own deceit

When blinded by pain

I know you weren't strong enough for that

Or to say you knew it, too

Cookware

Hues can speak
Pick me, pick me they beg the glazer
Who's tasked with cooking up a cheerful shade,
Something a housewife will love

Enamel over cast iron
Good for stewing and simmering
Like the woman at the stove

The deep orange at the bottom
Lightens as it climbs
The band in the middle
A tropical sunset

Not that she'd know

Too many colors there for her taste
Everything in black and white

Do, don't, in, out, yes, no

Simpler that way

Hard lines hold us up

That pot holds her subtler self

The one who blends and softens

But only with a recipe

Never another human heart

The dishes she made

The stuff of legend

Grief

Sit

Weep yourself dry
For the coming loss
And falling light

Wind rises,
Then stills

Believe in mercy,
Pray for peace

Open your heart to
Unseen years

Walk the earth she
Lies in

Carry her in the place

Surrendered the moment

She came into view

After That

She stands tall to water the hanging plant

Can too small, soil so dry

Back to the outside faucet she goes

For a refill

Her son still dead

The one driving still not

For years dreams were lies

He's at practice

He'll be home before dark

Then they were a single word

No no no no no no no

Waking hours buried below

Chores and duties

After that, just exhaustion

Grief the daily landscape,

Death the narrow path toward night

Diary of a False Assassin

It starts with love or a lot of like

He's crazy cute, right?

He'll say anything to make you let him

It takes you by surprise

Even though you know how it works

Hoping it wouldn't ≠a plan to prevent it

You don't tell anyone

Then you tell everyone

Have it, don't have it

Here's the number of the clinic

I'll drive you, myself

It's out-of-state

If you don't have it, you're a murderer

Puzzle of the day: if that thing in your stomach

Has no brain and no heart, why is it more

Important than you?

Because you have no value

Except to bear things

You're an incubator

An earthen vessel

And now, with a thought to your

Own future, a killing machine

A false assassin

About Anne Leigh Parrish

Anne Leigh Parrish is the author of fifteen books, including short stories, novels, and poetry. She is passionate about women's rights, the fate of the planet, and the magic of long-term relationships. She has recently ventured into the art of photography. Learn more about her at anneleighparrish.com and at her photography website at laviniastudios.com. She lives in the South Sound Region of Washington State.

About Unsolicited Press

Unsolicited Press is based out of Portland, Oregon and focuses on the works of the unsung and underrepresented. As a womxn-owned, all-volunteer small publisher that doesn't worry about profits as much as championing exceptional literature, we have the privilege of partnering with authors skirting the fringes of the lit world. We've worked with emerging and award-winning authors such as Ay Shimshon-Santo, Heather Lang-Cassera, John W. Bateman, Douglas Cole, Elisa Carlsen, and Sung J. Woo.

Learn more at unsolicitedpress.com. Find us on instagram, X, bsky, threads, youtube, facebook, and pinterest.

www.ingramcontent.com/pod-product-compliance
Lightning Source LLC
Chambersburg PA
CBHW031412120626
46545CB00006B/2119